T0145308

HANDBOOK FOR BEGINNERS OF SPIRITUAL

AND

PSYCHIC DEVELOPMENT

SHIRLEY M JANOVIC

Balboa Press books may be ordered through booksellers or by contacting:

Balboa Press
A Division of Hay House
1663 Liberty Drive
Bloomington, IN 47403
www.balboapress.com
1 (877) 407-4847

ISBN: 978-1-5043-1409-1 (sc)
ISBN: 978-1-5043-1408-4 (e)

Print information available on the last page.

Balboa Press rev. date: 07/30/2018

BALBOA
PRESS
A DIVISION OF HAY HOUSE

I believe that everyone is born with some form of psychic ability, and that they use it, completely unaware that they are doing so.

This book takes the magic out of being psychic and allows you to learn the basic language used by psychics. So that you may attend a meditation or development circle with a basic knowledge that I feel all people should have before starting on a journey of research.

Learn how to use the energies that psychics use.

Have you always wanted to know if you are psychic?

Do you have prophetic dreams or know who is on the phone before you answer it?

Have you always wanted to know how to meditate and what happens in a meditation or development circle?

Do you want to learn how to cleanse your home of negative energies?

It is my wish, that you continue your search, with the awareness, knowledge, and truth, that you receive here.

TABLE OF CONTENTS

I have found in my search towards higher Spiritual truths and Psychic Development, that the basics, are often overlooked. Most people go straight into a development circle or meditation group, without knowing what the basics are. Then, they tend to flounder and feel overwhelmed, because they don't know the little things, such as:

Why do we need protection?
How do we put protection around ourselves?
What is a guide?
What is an aura?
What are chakras?

and so on. What I am endeavoring to do in this handbook, is to give those people who are wanting to learn about meditation and Spiritual and psychic development, the tools and information, that I believe should be given to **ALL** people, who have decided to lift their energies and develop their Spiritual and Psychic abilities, so that they have a basic knowledge to fall back on. Knowing how I felt when I first started to learn over 40 years ago and how vulnerable I was, I believe people stop their search, thinking that it is all too much trouble.

In this book, you will find only those terms and information, which I believe to be true. This book, I might add, is for beginners, so that hopefully you may go on with the basic knowledge I feel is needed to continue without fear, to bigger and better research for yourself.

ENERGY

We are all made up of energy, there are no exceptions. Everything and everybody is the same. Whether it is a human being, an animal, a tree, or any other inanimate object. Another name for this energy is "Prana" or "Chi". We also have an energy field around us, as you will probably know if you have seen any aura photography. The more you become aware of the energy you possess, and learn to work with it, the easier it will be to tune into your spiritual and psychic abilities. For energy is your key to development. Now the big question is "how do you become aware of this energy and build it up? You build it with:

Meditation

You will need to meditate daily, if you are to lift your energies and expand your aura, to enable your guides to communicate with you. In doing this, you will feel calmer and less stressed about everyday problems. Things that used to annoy you will do so no longer and you will find that you are happier and more able to feel the energies around and within you.

Self-Discipline

It is very important that you discipline yourself to continue with your development, even if you do not get the results you want, as quickly as you feel you should. Some people need a little bit longer to develop, then others. So, don't be discouraged.

Belief in Yourself

If you do not believe what you get through in meditation, or when you get messages from spirit, you will put a stop, on any communications you receive. When you believe in what comes through, (no matter how silly it sounds to you, at the time), you allow the flow of communication to continue. You can liken it to turning on a tap. When you turn on a tap, you allow the water to flow, but when you turn the tap off, the water stops flowing. The same thing happens when you receive messages from spirit. You receive the message and think it's right, but if you then start to doubt, you will find that the flow will stop, and your communication will cease.

PROTECTION

One of the first things you need to learn about is protection. This is not because something bad can happen to you if you meditate or begin to develop. It is because when you start to develop, you may "pick up" from others around you. You might think "well that's what I want to learn, so what's the problem". Let me give you a common example. Have you ever gone into a supermarket, feeling relaxed and enjoying the idea of doing your shopping? You have your list and you know you have enough money to cover the cost of what you intend to buy. But within a short time, you find yourself feeling upset, confused, and worried. Wondering if you have enough money to pay for your purchases. You become tense and insecure. You may even feel a headache coming on. This is because you have come into contact with some people in the Supermarket, who are worried about what they are buying, and if they have enough money to pay for their purchases. They may also be wondering how they are going to afford to pay their bills etc. Because of this they may have a headache as well. All of which you maybe "picking up" and carrying around with you, thinking it is all yours. Sound familiar? Yes. This is the reason why you need to put protection around yourself. So that you don't pick up the negative energies from other people.

How we do this

The easiest way to put protection around yourself is to visualize, or if you can't visualize, just think of a beautiful white light in front of you. You can feel the warmth and love within it. Now step into that light. Feel it wrap itself around you. Know that it will protect you from any negative thoughts or actions that you may encounter.

The real protection in this little visualization is the **intention** of your action. The **INTENTION** is the main aspect that will completely protect you.

The more you practice this the easier it will become and the more you will feel protected.

FEAR

The main thing to remember here is that, **"LIKE ATTRACTS LIKE".** If you are fearful of developing your spiritual and psychic abilities, you will attract what you fear. This is in **ALL** things in life, not only spiritual and psychic development, but here, we are only talking about your spiritual and psychic development. There is nothing that can hurt you except your own fear. So, your first lesson is to let go of your fear. I have found that fear is generated mainly from lack of knowledge. What you don't know you fear. Once you gain the knowledge, your fears should drop away. Of course, we all have fears, it is quite normal, but before starting any development you should work on letting go of any fears you have, about developing your spiritual and psychic abilities. Know that you are in control at all times and do not allow fear to enter. Spiritual and psychic development is very natural. If you are unable to do this at this time, I suggest that you delay your learning until you are able to develop without fear.

CLEANSING

By cleansing, I mean getting rid of any unwanted energies, or feelings of negativity, within yourself or your home. These cleansings may work on your aura and chakras as well as your body. Here are some of the ways you can do this.

Visualization

Visualize a white light in the centre of your room, or if you are cleansing yourself, in the centre of your chest. Then allow the light to grow bigger and bigger until your whole room or body is filled with the white light, and as it does your **intention** should be that your room or body is cleansed of all negative energies, and unwanted feelings, that were within the room, or your body. Remember the **INTENTION** is the key to this cleansing.

Smudging

Smudging is similar to visualization, except that you hold the smudging stick in your hand, and allow the smoke to work in the corners, as well as the room itself. Once again it is with intention that the cleansing takes place. Smudging sticks may be bought at your store or online.

Reiki/Spiritual Healing

There are many forms of healing that you may use for cleansing as well. Reiki and Spiritual Healing are the two most common forms. Reiki is a hands-on healing method and can use different kinds of energy. The Reiki practitioner is able, to cleanse and heal with these energies. Spiritual Healing can also be hands on, or off, depending on how the practitioner giving the healing/cleansing operates with their guide and energy.

Crystals

There are many crystals that can be used for cleansing, healing and protection. One way these are used, is on your chakras (we will go into this in a later chapter). Other ways you can use the crystals, is to program them for cleansing (healing or protection or whatever you want them to do). One of my favourite crystals is Amethyst which is a good all-rounder for cleansing, healing and protection.

Crystals can be a very useful tool. You will find that there are many books on this subject, at your library or store.

Incense/Oil

These are another way of cleansing your home. Burning Sandalwood or Lemongrass incense or oil, are only two of the cleansers available. You may buy these at your store or on line.

Another way of cleansing yourself of any negativity, is to stand under a shower, and as the water washes over your head and body, imagine all your problems and negativity washing down the drain with it.

Once again (and I cannot say this enough times) you must remember that your **intention** is the main object of these cleansings.

GUIDES

Everyone has a guide. Some people call them guardian angels. Some call them spirit people. Others may call them guides, healers or helpers. There are those who refer to them as their mother, father or great aunt Bess, who has passed over into the spirit world. Whatever you wish to call them, they are with you constantly. You are never left alone. They are here to guide you through life and steer you in the direction that you are meant to go. They will prompt you and put blocks in front of you if you step off your path. When you are on the right path, they will push you forward, and help you all the way. The way you will know if you are on the right path is that generally, everything will flow without hassle.

There are all kinds of guides. Your personal spirit guide is with you from before you are born, until after you die. There are healing guides that you can call on to help you, with the healing of yourself or others. There are other guides also, to help you with anything that you wish to do or learn. There are no boundaries on their help, it is limitless. You just need to remember to ask, and you will receive all the help you need.

AURAS

As I have said before everyone and everything is energy. Each one of us, all animals and inanimate objects, are surrounded by an energy field, which shows itself in colour to those who are able to see. This is called an "aura". This field can be seen pulsating and changing colours as your emotions and life change. It can also be felt and sensed. It is through practice that you are able to see it. You are also able to cleanse and heal through the aura. Each of the colours in the aura have a different meaning, some of which are.

Red: passion or anger
Orange: creativity
Blue: emotional/spiritual growth
Green: physical healing and growth
Yellow: mental and intellectual
Violet: wisdom/love

See pictures of auras taken with an aura photography camera

CHAKRAS

Chakras are the Spiritual energy centre's in the body. There are seven main chakras. With these you are able to heal, cleanse, balance and ground yourself. Each chakra has a different colour and works in different ways. I have outlined here a short list of the chakra colours, the location on the body and how you can work with them. I have also included a diagram of the chakras. You will learn more about the chakras and how to use them when you attend a development circle. Other avenues of learning are from books at your library or store.

Root/base chakra: red   at the base of the spine

It is with this chakra that you can ground yourself and work on to stabilize your life and gain material and financial things in life.

Sacral chakra: orange   approx. two inches below the naval.

You can work on this chakra when you want to learn anything, on a creative level.

Solar plexus: yellow   under the diaphragm.

This chakra rules the intellectual aspects. If you are studying, you can work on this chakra. You may also benefit from sitting in a room with yellow light.

Heart chakra: green   middle of the chest.

This chakra represents love, compassion and connection with others.

Throat chakra: blue   middle of the throat.

This is the chakra you work on if you have trust issues. You may also want to work on this chakra if you are afraid of speaking in front of people.

Brow chakra: indigo   middle of the brow.

This represents your vision and intuition.

Crown chakra: violet   crown of the head.

This is where you connect with your Divine Source/God/Creator.

I have also added the name of some crystals that may be used on the chakras for cleansing and healing.

Root chakra	-	Hematite
Sacral chakra	-	Citrine
Solar Plexus chakra	-	Malachite
Heart chakra	-	Rose Quartz
Throat chakra	-	Lapis Lazuli
Third Eye chakra	-	Amethyst
Crown chakra	-	Clear Quartz

You should be able to learn how to use these chakras when you attend a Spiritual and psychic development circle. As I have said before there are many books that you may also learn from at your library or store.

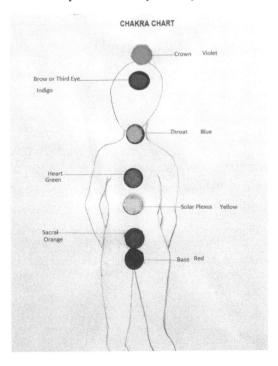

CHAKRA CHART

Crown   Violet

Brow or Third Eye
Indigo

Throat   Blue

Heart
Green

Solar Plexus   Yellow

Sacral
Orange

Base   Red

MEDITATION GROUP

This is where you lift your energies and connect with your spirit guides and the Divine/God. In doing this you will gain spiritual insights as well as psychic awareness. There are many forms of meditation, but the most common is, the guided meditation in which the leader of the group talks you through or you have an audio recording (which you may buy at your store or on line), with someone else talking you through. As the leader of the group talks and you listen, you may find that your thoughts wander. If this happens, don't try to stop the thought. Just allow it to come in, acknowledge that it is there, and then allow it to gently flow out. If you try to stop the thought you will only give that thought energy, and allow it to build up, so that you are unable to follow the meditation. Most people when they first start to meditate will see colours. This is very common. As you begin to meditate on a regular basis you will most probably see spirit and other things as well. One such spirit person may be your guide. Most people when they first start meditating think that everything they see is their own imagination. This is completely normal. Remember belief in yourself is one of the first lessons. Once you are able to believe in what you are getting through you will develop quicker. This will vary from person to person. I must add, that you should be comfortable with all the other sitters in the meditation group. If you find that you or they have issues, which make you feel anxious, I suggest that you find another group.

Daily meditation will calm you and change your life. You will become less stressed and more able to live your life in love and peace. Meditation is not religion based, even though we do ask the Divine/God for protection, we are not teaching or changing your mind about your religion. It will not change your personal religious beliefs unless you wish them to change. You can (and most people do) continue to practice their own religious beliefs as well as using meditation as another tool to uplift their energies and heighten their connection with their Divine/God.

I have given you a small meditation here, that you may practice. Have someone read it to you so that you can relax and flow with it.

Meditation in Space

As you sit comfortably in your chair, I want you to imagine a beautiful white light washing over your feet and legs, and as it does it drains away all the tension that you are storing in your muscles. Feel the warmth of the light, feel how relaxed your feet and legs are becoming. And as they become even more relaxed, this beautiful white light makes its way up into your body and arms, allowing this part of your body to relax. Feel it relax. Let it relax. Your feet, your legs, your body and arms are all loose, relaxed and comfortable. The light now flows gently up into your neck and head. Feel all the muscles in your neck relaxing, and all the tension in your head flowing out, leaving you completely relaxed and comfortable, and as your body relaxes even more, the white light goes higher and higher, taking you with it. Up, up into the atmosphere, up into the darkness of space. Feel how relaxed you are as you journey onward and upward, higher and higher you go, up towards your Divine/God, knowing that you are completely safe, enjoying your new experience. I will let you flow on now with your new freedom and will bring you back shortly........................... (10minutes)

It is now time for you to come back. I want you to remember all that you have seen and all that you have heard and bring it back with you. Allow yourself to gently float back down, into the atmosphere, and down through the clouds, down, down you come, gently coming back into your chair. Feel your body returning to your chair. Now open your eyes.

DEVELOPMENT CIRCLE

At a development circle, you will not only meditate but will be taught how to use the energies that will come with your Spiritual and psychic development. When you choose a development circle, there should be a good rapport between the people. In this way you will develop quicker, as the energies will be more intense and compatible. If there is friction between any of the sitters in the circle for any reason, you will find that the energies will only build to the level of that negativity. Because you will be meditating, and your senses will be enhanced, you will need to know that you are sitting within a positive atmosphere. So, you see why it is so important that you select the right circle. If you sit in a group for a couple of times, you should know whether it is compatible with you. If you find that it is not, you will need to find another group. You will not develop sitting in a group where you do not feel comfortable.

You will usually find that the leader of the circle will first sit you in a straight-back chair to start. When everyone is seated, she then proceeds to say a short prayer and ask for protection for all the people there. With this done she will start the meditation. This usually comprises of a small relaxation exercise. Then a guided meditation, in which she will take you on a journey for a short time, after which she will tell you to carry on and will bring you back to your chair after you have had some time meditating. She will then ask you what you saw or heard whilst you were in meditation and will attempt, to give you an explanation for whatever you received. After she has finished her explanations for all the sitters, she will most likely then ask you to do some psychometry. This is explained in the next chapter.

Don't worry if you don't get anything, as this is not unusual for people just starting meditation. The more you meditate the easier it becomes and the more you will receive.

MEDIUMS

There are many forms of mediumship. Every person who gives messages from spirit is a medium. As in all professions, there are many levels of mediumship, some excellent, and some not so excellent, and a lot in-between.

Trance/Channel Mediums

A trance medium is a person who is able to channel spirit and allows them to then take over her own body. This spirit, can be a guide, someone's relative, which has passed over etc., or a guide who can teach or heal others, such as Ester Hicks who channels "Abraham". There are also mediums who can produce ectoplasm, which is a substance that builds up into a spirit person. This particular type of medium is very rare today.

Clairvoyants

Clairvoyants are mediums who see and hear spirit, either subjectively or objectively. By this I mean, that they can see and hear in their mind (mentally) which is subjectively, or physically (as you would see the person next to you) which is objectively. They then proceed to give the messages they are receiving.

Psychometry

With this a medium holds an object of the sitters' and feels the energy within it. In this way she can "pick up" information and pass it onto the sitter. This is usually what is taught in a meditation or development circle and is one of the easiest the learn.

Automatic Writing

With this Spirit takes over the hand/arm of the medium and writes that which they wish to say. With this the person who has allowed Spirit to use her is not able to write anything herself. Spirit is completely in control of her arm/hand and everything that is written.

Inspirational Writing

Inspirational writing may be received through the mind. The medium then writes down that which is perceived from spirit. This type of communication generally comes through very quickly and is one of the easiest to achieve. This type of communication can come through as verse as well.

Example: *We shall talk of love. Not the love of the physical body but the love of the soul. The real love. The love which is life. The true meaning of each and every person. This love is beyond some for they do not strive. They are content with the physical and do not want to work for the higher spiritual love of which they are entitled. Why my children. It is yours for the taking. Pick up the veil and glance but for a moment at that which you so cheerfully turn your back on. With this love to turn to, the soul is always at peace. This is the medicine of the spirit. The true spirit.*

Clairaudience

With clairaudience the medium receives messages from spirit through the ear. I'm sure you have all heard of Doris Stokes who received messages in this way. The medium then proceeds to give the sitter the messages she has heard.

Inspirational Poetry

With this spirit gives poetry to the medium through the mind, the same as inspirational writing. The only difference is, that the communication comes through in verse as the medium writes it down.

Example: **THE SMALL WHITE LIGHT**

Like a small white light, it grows within
Showering your being with all it can
The light grows gently and as it does
Your life brightens up like a new born dove
The sun shines brighter, and the world seems new
The happiness within you is elevated too
But what you have found is not unknown
Many others have reached it, you are not alone
Great numbers search for the key to life
And great numbers find it in this small white light

Psychic Art

With psychic art, the medium is able to draw or paint spirit people etc., (with whatever type of art medium she prefers), the medium once again may receive images or may have inspiration as to where to put the paint, or other medium that they are using, and which colours to use. See the example of a Spirit Guide that was drawn by a psychic artist.

"STANDING CLOUD"

With all these different kinds of mediumship, it is always with the full consent of the medium that the communications are achieved. Spirit never takes over or uses a medium without the medium's full consent.

HEALING

Healing can be done by anyone wishing to help another person. Giving a person a hug is a form of healing. Listening to someone is also a form of healing when a friend or even a stranger, needs to talk. There are so many forms of healing it would be impossible to note them all here.

A few of the most common ones are Spiritual healing, Reiki, Reflexology and Massage.

Spiritual Healing

This can be done by anyone who knows about energies. With this the practitioner will use the energy of spirit to heal, which is directed through the hands into the patient. With this healing you will generally feel the energy as it is being poured into your body. This energy is usually warm but may occasionally also be cool. A lot of patients after having this type of healing may become tearful because the energies work on the emotions, as well as the physical body. If the patient has a physical problem which is not healed, you will usually find that she has gained emotional balance and has changed her attitude towards the problem.

Reiki

This type of healing is similar to Spiritual healing except it usually uses a hands-on approach. With Reiki, the practitioner can use different symbols and energies, which can be very powerful. The Reiki practitioner uses the symbols and directs her energies through her hands and into the patient. Again, this type of healing can work on the emotions as well as the physical body and the patient can feel tearful after a session.

Reflexology

Reflexology is massage and pressure on different points of the feet which is said to represent the different parts of the body. The patient usually has sore spots relating to the area that needs healing within the body. It is very relaxing and usually you find that you are feeling much better after it.

Massage

I am sure that most of you are aware of massage. If you haven't had one already, you are missing out on a natural way of healing and cleansing. Massage is a very good way of healing and releasing toxins within the body. As the therapist massages she allows her healing energies to penetrate the body. This is generally called an "exchange of energy". After a healing massage you will not only feel good but will usually be filled with energy and calmness.

With all healing, I have found that the more compassion you have for your patient the more healing energy you will be able to generate, and the more intense the energies are. If you are healing someone, you should **never** use your own energy. You will know if you are, as you will feel extremely tired and will be unable to continue for long periods of time.

All healing energies come from spirit and not from the healers themselves. All healers are only the channels for spirit.

Listen to all that is given to you both physically and psychically – accept only what you feel to be right for you at the time (this will change over the years so don't be afraid to think for yourself) and leave the rest behind.

There are no limits

The only limits for you are the ones you impose on yourself

Printed in the United States
By Bookmasters